Susan Terris

GREATEST
HITS
1980-2000

Susan Terris $8.95
GREATEST HITS 1980-2001
Greatest Hits Series #1   ISBN 1-930755-02-3

Copyright © 2000 2002 Susan Terris
All rights reserved. Pudding House retains permission to reprint.
To copy any of these poems individually, permission
must first be obtained from the author in writing.
SECOND EDITION
Printed in the United States of America

Pudding House Publications
60 North Main Street
Johnstown Ohio 43031
740-967-6060
pudding@johnstown.net
www.puddinghouse.com

ACKNOWLEDGMENTS

"Onions"—*MacGuffin*; "Green Shade"—*The Spoon River Poetry Review;*
"Applesauce"—*Poetry Now*; "Camera Obscura"—*Inkwell Magazine*; "Boxcar At The
Holocaust Museum"—*Many Mountains Moving;* "Fugue State"—*Kansas
Quarterly/Arkansas Review*; "The Woman On Death Row Watches TV"—*Clackamas
Literary Review;* "Afterimages"—*Salt Hill*, Muse Press; "Hester Prynne's Grammar: A
Lesson In Tense"—*Poetry Northwest*; "Molly Bloom Has The Last Word"—*Iowa Woman*;
"Forgiveness"—*The Sow's Ear Poetry Review*

PRIZE-WINNING POEMS & POEMS CITED FOR SPECIAL MERIT

"Boxcar At The Holocaust Museum"—1st Prize 1996 *Noe Valley Voice* Poetry
    Competition, 1st Prize 1997 *Many Mountains Moving* Poetry Competition
"Afterimages"—1st Prize 1997 Muse Press Broadside Competition, 1st Prize 1998 *Salt Hill*
    Poetry Competition
"Camera Obscura"—2nd Prize 1997 *Inkwell Magazine* Poetry Competition
"Molly Bloom Has The Last Word"—2nd Prize 1994 *Iowa Woman* Poetry Competition
"Forgiveness," "The Woman On Death Row Watches TV," and "Onions" won prizes or
    were finalists in poetry competitions sponsored by: *The Sow's Ear Poetry Review,
    Clackamas Literary Review, UAS Explorations,* and *The MacGuffin.*

"Forgiveness" appeared in the following anthologies: *Claiming the Spirit Within*, Beacon
    Press, 1996, and *Words & Quilts*, The Quilt Digest Press, 1996.

Some of the poems have been published in the following books by Susan Terris: *Curved
    Space*, La Jolla Poets Press, 1998; *Eye of the Holocaust*, Arctos Press, 1999; *Killing in
    the Comfort Zone*, Pudding House Publications, 1995.

Publisher's Position Statement
on the Value of Poetry Arts

This chapbook is limited edition fine art
from the poet

Susan Terris

whose work you support for a few cents per page.
You are not buying paper and printer's ink by
weight. You selected language art that took as long
to create as paintings or other fine art. Pudding
House caters to those who understand the value of
the poet's good work. We are in business to
enhance reputations rather than to assure profits for
our press. Poets are chosen for this project on the
basis of their contribution to literary arts and to the
popular culture.

On behalf of a large community of
contemporary poets, this poet in particular, and
Pudding House Publications, thank you for
supporting this project.

Susan Terris
GREATEST HITS
1980–2000

Table of Contents

About Susan Terris

Susan Terris' first full-length book *Curved Space* was published in 1998 (La Jolla Poets Press). In 1999, she had two books published: *Eye of the Holocaust* (Arctos Press) and *Angels of Bataan* (Pudding House Publications).

Other recent books are: *Killing in the Comfort Zone* (Pudding House Publications) and *Nell's Quilt* (Farrar, Straus & Giroux). Her journal publications include *The Antioch Review, The Midwest Quarterly, Ploughshares, Missouri Review, Nimrod,* and *The Southern California Anthology.* In 1998, 1999, and 2000, Ms. Terris was nominated for Pushcart Prizes. She also won first place in 6 poetry competitions, and was a 2nd place winner or finalist in 20 other national competitions.

Ms. Terris lives in San Francisco with her husband, David.

The Echo Of Memory

After a 25-year career as a writer of fiction (21 books published by Farrar, Straus & Giroux, Doubleday, Macmillan) and sometime published poet, I've made a career change and am now writing and publishing only poetry. In the last 10 years, I have had more than 300 poems published in journals and magazines, had poems in 14 national anthologies, and have had *Curved Space* (La Jolla Poets Press, 1998), my first full-length book of poems, published.

The 12 poems in this chapbook are, I think, the best of my performance poems as well as the ones most often requested for reprints. The first, "Onions," is a favorite opener for readings and was a break-through poem for me, one of the first where I found a comfortable way to write about personal secrets. The second, "Green Shade" is one of my daughter poems. My sons often wonder why they don't appear as often on the printed page; but I think for a woman the experience of *being* a daughter as well as having a daughter provides endless amounts of material to ponder. This poem was actually written about the daughter of a friend, though my own daughter persists in imagining it's about her.

"Camera Obscura" was another turning point in my work. It represented the beginning of my interest in linking disparate ideas as well as the beginning of a need to create less linear, more surreal poems. It's also one of my marriage poems. "Applesauce," which follows it, is a more succinct comment on marriage; and I've included it here to show—that despite much evidence to the contrary—I do write some short poems. It is also the first poem I ever had published.

"Boxcar At The Holocaust Museum," on the other hand, is a narrative poem, one part of a long sequence that forms the center section of my chapbook *Eye of the Holocaust* (Arctos Press, 1999). An emotional piece, this often leaves me and my audiences feeling a little shaky. "Boxcar" is just one of the poems I've written over the years that have to do with murder in one way or another. Twenty-eight of them, including "Fugue State," were included in a 1996 Pudding House chapbook called *Killing in the Comfort Zone*. "The

Woman On Death Row Watches TV" is a newer poem that falls into this same category. The winter before Karla Fay Tucker was executed, the eastern half of the United States was hit by a particularly vicious storm. Karla Fay Tucker and the storm came together in this poem. It's one of many I've written where the inspiration was originally a newspaper article.

Then there are the persona poems and the love poems. I've done a large number of these—including several dozen in the voices of women from famous works of literature. Two of my favorites are "Hester Prynne's Grammar" and "Molly Bloom Has The Last Word." I frequently use the Molly poem to close a reading; but in this volume where she's the 10th out of 12 poems, she does not get to have the last word. The piece that follows Molly's is another love poem, one that has won several prizes, and another poem, inspired by a quote from artist Ivan Albright, where I deal with more abstract material.

"Forgiveness" is probably the most reprinted poem of all my work. It is again surreal and tries to say something about creativity and being a creative person. The last poem in this volume, a newer abstract and surreal piece, addresses the nature of what is real and what is not, what is true and what is not, a question frequently asked of me and of other poets. My conclusion:

"Everything here is true. Everything false.

This is the lie of memory. Muscle of memory.

Arrogance of memory. Echo of memory."

—Susan Terris

ONIONS

Potatoes would grow behind my ears,
they said, if I didn't wash
and radishes beneath my fingernails,
onions beneath arms, corn between toes,
carrots amid the sheep's-path of my part.
Watermelon vines and apple trees would
flourish within from seeds
swallowed as I ate too fast,
careless of details as I was with
all aspects of a fragile, corporeal self.
Inside my nose or navel,
between my legs were other unclean places
no one mentioned, freeing me to suspect
leeks, chives, parsley, wild mustard,
as I probed with curious fingers, tasted.

A sly, secretive child dedicated to sowing
seeds of sedition, I reveled that
my alien, vinegar-onion-sweat-scented
green-brown body could contain seeds.
Woody, potato-eyed, sporting tubers,
fronds, vines, stalks, blossoms over
layer within translucent layer, I raced.
And then, tying sashes of smocked dresses
high to simulate pregnancy,
I marched in measured cadences,
convinced that fruit and vegetable pips
cached now in my womb and at other sites
would someday germinate to produce
round—if still unclean and reeking—creatures:
strange-bright mirror-image selves.

GREEN SHADE

Kneeling alone in a chill orchard, you shake branches
and gather windfall. Beware—*a green thought
in a green shade*—of what you wish for.
In the tentative way women are conditioned
to ask for the things they want, you wished for
a daughter; and, yes, she seemed
perfect; so how could you suspect
olive eyes, pale skin, tufts of tangled hair?

You sent her along wild paths, offered the chase,
rush of blood sport. Later, she sank milk-fangs
in your throat and began to drink. Had you
seen signs, understood ungovernable impulses,
menace under soft flesh, you might have
strung garlic cloves about your neck
or sought a midnight crossroads to drive a stake
through her heart. *Too cruel*, you say,
much too cruel? Bone of your bones, flesh of your flesh:
instead, you've let her suck you dry.
Now while you succumb, she grows,

scorning the weakness which nourishes her.
This victory is Pyrrhic; for today—near-orphan—
she wails of abuse and abandonment. Mothers, daughters.
Daughters, mothers. You know you must warn others,
teach them to sniff out rot
below girls' sweet apple-cheeks; but, green shade,
you kneel waiting for blood
to pool and let down so she can, once more, latch on.

APPLESAUCE

A married woman's kitchen—
essence of ammonia and Comet cleanser,
crumbs gone stale from last week's brownies
left unfoiled upon the tiles,
a time warp of Hansel's crusts
strewn from
peanut butter sandwiches;
yet, still, in the basket of the Foley food mill—
apples,
a hopeful nosegay of puckered apples
being pressed into familiar, sweet-smelling
applesauce.

Camera Obscura

She waits in darkness staring down
at the parabola of wave, sand, gull, and rock.
Views shift clockwise and clockwise, breakers siphon
off the curved lip, until the world
is upside-down yet circling to re-right itself.
A pelican skids, beaks a fish, wings over the rim
of the silken bowl. A thin woman dressed
in black, who might be herself, descends stairs
and vanishes in the Musée Mechanique.

Leonardo knew this camera. Vermeer used it
for portraits: a spinning mirror
and lenses—one convex, one concave.
As light glints through an aperture,
a picture roils upon a curve in a dim room.
Standing there watching her spouse and children
rotate out of sight on the beach below,
she feels herself begin to invert
and slide off the surface into nothingness

or coexistence. Leaving the camera, she climbs
to the street and a car hits her. Standing at the curb,
she sees a car hit someone else.
She steps in front of a car and no impact jars.
But maybe she never moved at all. Music, odd and
cymbal-like, dins her head. Moments peel off: history
of what happens or what might be. Perhaps she
can choose memory. Elect the outcome,
dismiss the accident, moment of rape or desertion.

Her children, robust and long-limbed, cavort
yet orbit off the smooth edges
of the arc. Each rotation they are changed,
color-leached, flatter, more distant.
Her husband riffles pages of his paper yet stares
outward toward the breaker line where a windsurfer
luffs a waxy sail. This man with newspaper
is a white-haired stranger in polar fleece.
She might abandon the dark room and meet him
on the beach. She might, like the woman in black,
glide into the Musée, face Laughing Sal's
day-glo ringlets and lewd-jiggle cantaloupe breasts.
Or she may risk the path of the oncoming car,
cross the street and dissolve,
leaving everything and everyone
capsized in the oceanic curve of time.

Boxcar At The Holocaust Museum

Assaulted by brick and steel, my sister and I cross
the glass bridge between then and now, touch
Szumsk, the Polish town
our grandparents came from, walk into
Ejszyszki Tower eyeing photo doppelgängers
of relatives we call the monkey aunts,
of an uncle who couldn't skate the '36 Olympics,
of our parents, ourselves.

My younger sister has married a Baptist, raised
children who don't believe they are Jews;
yet she—riveted—is moving snail's-pace.
So when I come upon it, I am alone.
It's an old red cattle car like those from
our Missouri childhood, counted as they
clacked by full of livestock
due for slaughter. But this one is different.
To avoid passing through, I pretend
to examine oxidized razors, forks,
tea strainers, then metal instruments
of torture which up-close
become umbrella frames. I check my watch,
consider flight...

                        yet as I turn, I see my sister
by the boxcar unwilling to enter. *Why are
we here?* Hurrying toward her, I move past
cart, suitcases, hat boxes. *What will it tell us?*
For a moment, we are side by side, aware of

primal, physical comfort. Then together
we step in. It is dark. We do not
speak. After 50 years, stench still saturates
the boards. As I inhale it, I feel fingers
tug at the pleats of my skirt,
at my sweater, my hands. Sweaty heads
I can't see butt me, begging for refuge,
those who would not have been spared:
my children, my sister's Mischling children,
my own Mischling grandchildren.

Suddenly, a soprano voice echoes around us.
Choo-choo. Turning, we see a boy-child
havened between parents.
He smiles, nods sweetly, beckoning to us and to
the invisible hordes pressed close. *Choo-choo,*
he repeats. *Choo-choo. All aboard...*

FUGUE STATE

She is in a fugue state. There are holes
in her arm made by the fat man with suitcase
and Uzzi. As her husband, a red blossom spreading across
his chest, lies in her lap, she hears screams
and mewling. A swift—if imperfect—shield,
he'd wedged his body in front of hers.
Now while she cries, odd sounds
chirr from his throat.
She feels burning, numbness; and when she looks up,
tinted windows of his office
pewter the sky.
Somehow, he'd punched an outside line
so she could plead for help.
Now, though time creeps, they wait.
I'm dying, he manages, as cones from spotlights
sear, *and we need to say good-bye.*

This is only shock, she tells herself. Help
will come. Things will be all right.
We'll have children and beachcomb in Kauai.

Week-old tulips, ones she'd bought
for his birthday, gape in the crystal bowl
atop the desk. They are scarlet,
yet not as scarlet as the bouquet mantling his shirt.
Nothing again will ever be real, she murmurs.
I am beyond the rainbow.
Today is yesterday inside out. Tomorrow

is upside down. I was young, and now I am old,
because there are holes in him. In me, too:
both of us are leaking.
If there were holes in time, I would inch
backwards with him, babe in my arms,
seal them over, lullaby us into yesterday.
Or I would tell him how the wizard told the sultan
the earth is held up on the back of
a giant elephant, and the elephant stands on
the back of a giant turtle. After that,
of course, it's turtles—turtles, all the way down...

For them, the past was always overture. But now
his parched lips snap, turtle-like yet mute;
and past is everything, for she is in a fugue state.

THE WOMAN ON DEATH ROW WATCHES TV

Live wires arc and burn in snow. Branches are encased in ice.
They snap and shatter into devil's fingers. This spring,
willow trees, their limbs sheared, will have no leaves.
She sees herself, too, on TV. Her warm face spliced
with trees cracking, falling on cars, on houses. People are
frosted to the bone. Feet numb yet they struggle to endure
the killing cold. But others will die. They have no
water, no heat, no light. She prays for them.

Cold through the veins. That, they say, is the first thing
a person feels. A snake inching its way toward the heart.
An ice that burns. Then twitches, jerks, a cough.
A high keening noise. Silence. A doctor with a stethoscope.
And this will happen soon, injection in a frozen moment,
because she was a violent girl, wild with drugs, who wielded
an axe. But, in prison, she grew up, unthawed, tried on
beauty and God. Too late, she became someone else.

In the TV glacier, skeletons of boar and woolly mammoth
cradled as part of a slow-moving river that compresses
ice to dense, uncanny marble. Other bones, those of a girl
a thousand years old, lie with them, skin shriveled to leather,
body shrouded in dreamless sleep, limbs unmoving and fetus
cocooned in her belly. She'd been godless, perhaps, immune
to rules, someone who'd killed or maimed cast in alive.
And there, in a blue crevasse, she'd clawed against oblivion.

Hypothermia. Not from an inching glacier but falling into
chilled water like she saw in the trailer for *Titanic.*
Needles of pain, choked breath, and delirium. Burning below
in a too-cold cave where all air has been sucked out by fire.
This is a pagan hell. Styx is a river of ice. On Channel 9,
Charon steers a boat but, here, a sled. She's sheened with ice.
In some whiteout blizzard, she killed someone. More than one.
Now she burns and freezes. Life is here. No, it is not here.

Nor is God. Willows will have no leaves but fingers
of ice. No heat. No light. And they will die.

Hester Prynne's Grammar:
A Lesson In Tense

I lay my skirt across a chair and it lies there.
   (Present.)
I laid my slippers on the floor and they lay there.
   (Past.)
I have laid myself upon a quilt and I have lain there.
   (Perfect.)

He lays his pants by my skirt and they lie there.
   (Present.)
He laid his boots beside my slippers and they lay there.
   (Past.)
He has laid his body next to mine and it has lain there.
   (Perfect.)

Lay, lies,
laid, lay
laid, lain.
All quite grammatically correct and, still, it is not
the lay or laid that bothers him but the lies.

He may love to lie with me, yet to lie about me is for him
a tense not coped with in any text of standard usage.
   (Imperfect.)

AFTERIMAGES

Paint a picture with afterimages only with the first colors gone—only afterimages—and carry it so you have some 3rd and 4th afterimages. Study the aftercolors of any and all objects and only paint the aftercolor.

—Ivan Albright

Doorbell, door, corridor, rain-studded coat, face smooth, ears rough, neck arching, cheek-on-cheek, mouths, the weight of morning, heat and smoke, clothes twisted, quilt and spread, sheets twisted, mango ripe, music, coffee—first the image, then luster and refraction

and with the prime pigment gone, repaint, feel brush beneath ribs again and again until *doorbell coat-damp* bristles lose thrust, until a not-something is a scrim of something *knob twisted parquet patchwork quilt* that happened then *Puccini* again and again to a person *rumpled shirt empty cup corridor mouth ripe* who may have been you

like in the quilted field of Tuscan flowers: wine and song, ruby figs, snake grass and wild oats now sepiaed with time *mango skin buttercup bed-spread bottleneck tongue and groove* from bright emerald to moss to celadon to patina *claret to peach to blush to milk to water* muscle sleeked to bone *cheek-heat out-of-doors wild snake rough-smoke* color tints *parquet of morning* bleed into a faint patchwork

a negative grace, image over image, multiplicity *viola nude descending lip-music ripe oak and tannin bent lilac bells* light-streaks through prisms *rain-smoke* landscape of then and now *morning-weight arch after-taste* subtlety of nuance *damp-twisted grass aria* and the afterimage of afterimage of afterimage *hair-spreading quilt-rumple door coffee spill* eye-echoes known *sheet-music* yet never again felt *coda* as story becomes vignette becomes moment becoming pause and

hands morning door to corridor ears patched breath cheeks coffee to buff green to ripe face-saving fig-flesh oat-spilling light—bright to dim then dimmer *rain-studs* so shade *snake-smooth scent* so scumble and see it thin *butterfly tongue and mango-poppy arch of smoke* until afterimages all merge *singers* the center pales *wing-shiver heat-spread lips brushing* the aftercolor washes at margins *the singing* objects *door the song* objectivity *the verse* rods and color-wands *line bell vibrato* straw and shadow matter *the rough silence*

MOLLY HAS THE LAST WORD

Yes love lovers frigging sex the smell of a man
thats all anyone ever supposes I think about
dresses perfume flesh roses men getting up under
my petticoats and giving kisses
long and hot down to my soul and forget that like
other women I am sensitive can cry
yet you see I know more than most because of the word
because I read and have not only a soul but
gray matter too like the men
o rocks I dont know metempsychosis still with Calypso
barelolling above my brass bed I know winedark seas
have my own copy of Lord Byrons poems
as well as three pairs of gloves
lying here Ive read Wilkie Collins Moonstone
Rabelais East Lynne almost any book as long as it
hasnt a Molly in it
and bytheby have a passing acquaintance with Jane
Emma Tess Anna and some of their sisters
even if theyre all afraid to say what I say except
maybe Dame Alys of Bath for she like me is
yes earthy honest and somewhat taken with a bit of lace
a nice sort of brooch or young loins
and would know how to act when a man wanted to
milk her sweet and thick into his tea
but come from another time she hasnt had to listen to
bumgut filthyminded Dr Freud seen him kick up
a row trying to find out what it is women want
though he never asked me
yes of course I could have told him yes

for with my life and reading and knowing
women are sisters under their skins
this answers simple like the nose on his face and it is
power yes power we want
then people would be a fat lot better
and youd never see this much killing or drunkenness
so power it is in love in sex in war and you can
go all the way back if you wish to the ancient Greeks
to those sisters Fates Muses Seaside girls and the rest
yes they knew what they wanted as I know what I want
power but particularly the power
men have been least willing to give us
still with an Andalusian rose in my hair I will possess it
yes the power of the word
yes thats what women want yes the word yes

FORGIVENESS

Sometimes, I buy old quilts but never ones with any stain.
No tea, blood, or fluids that will not succumb to Tide.
This work, tendered by a woman from Missouri, is
Ocean Waves, 1890—white
with hand-dipped blue—loved, necessary.

A pattern both exuberant and contained, a triangulated
flow of motion. Yearning, I stretch my hands;
yet when we (the woman from Missouri and I) sail
the quilt outside on her line, there, borne on the crest
of a wave, is a mark. India ink. An exclamation point.

Indelible. The ink, I'm sure (men do not write in bed),
was dropped by a woman. Rorschached, I stare
until I see someone who dreamed oceans and words.
I know how, propped on pillows, fingers callused
from milking, stitch-pitted, she scrawled.
Alone at night, she stole
time to piece thoughts. But the quilt has

a stain. "No," I tell the woman from Missouri.
Still, that quilter, glances up from her tablet, squints
across time, summons me, alien of the future.
I do not move. Irked by my caution,
she gestures with her pen. A drop falls, leaving
a message that will last a hundred years.

"Stained," I murmur, undulated by Ocean Waves, glancing
toward the woman from Missouri. She's speaking,
but her words lap past as I (asking if anything of mine
will last a hundred years) hear only the other one,
the one with the pen. *Head, hand, heart,* she urges.
Courage. Eyes salted, I nod.
Then, for what we cannot change, I forgive us both.

Incoherence Of Time

Eddied until the continuum makes no sense:
branches that were bare tremble with leaves.
Dry streambeds run suddenly with water.

The child was by my side. She is under water.
She was in her bed. She is lost in a northern wood.
She was a child of light. She lives now in shadow.

Vases that held bouquets of fresh rosebuds
hold only stems and a scatter of puckered petals,
and the clear water has a soured yellow cast.

The apartment that was cold is on fire. It is
cinder and ash. The child had socks and shoes.
Now she has chilled feet and nightmares.

An hour vanishes in a breath. A month passes
between tonight's moonrise and moonset.
A bright necklace of hours beads into a year.

This morning, I was taut and lithe as the child.
But tonight my torso and feet are misshapen,
and I am too pain-throbbed to move at all.

Everything here is true. Everything false.
This is the lie of memory. Muscle of memory.
Arrogance of memory. The echo of memory.